DIGGING FOR TROY

TROY

From Homer to Hisarlik

Jill Rubalcaba *and* Eric H. Cline

with illustrations by Sarah S. Brannen

ii⌂i Charlesbridge

For Dan, Kelly, and Danny
—J. R.

For Diane, Hannah, Max, and Joshua
—E. H. C.

Acknowledgments
Books are collaborative efforts, and it has been our good fortune to have so many talented people working with us on this project. We'd like to express our gratitude to the following people who contributed generously to this project: first and foremost to our editor, Randi Rivers, for her tireless efforts digging through the layers of our manuscripts to uncover the Troy you see here. We owe the book's good looks to Diane Earley's art direction and design and to the photographic contributions from Cemal Pulak and the Institute of Nautical Archaeology at Texas A&M University, Peter Jablonka and the Troia Project at the University of Tübingen, Jack Davis, Carol Hershenson, and the Classics Department at the University of Cincinnati. And Nancy Hanger's meticulous copyediting kept us from going astray. Thanks to Ginger Knowlton for navigating the business end of things. And a special thanks to our families who encourage and support us in all our endeavors.

Photo on previous page: A bronze seal inscribed with a man's and woman's names found in level Troy VIIb at Hisarlik

Published by Charlesbridge
85 Main Street
Watertown, MA 02472
(617) 926-0329
www.charlesbridge.com

Library of Congress Cataloging-in-Publication Data
Cline, Eric H.
  Digging for Troy : from Homer to Hisarlik / Eric Cline and Jill Rubalcaba; illustrations by Sarah S. Brannen.
    p. cm.
  Includes index.
  ISBN 978-1-58089-326-8 (reinforced for library use)
  ISBN 978-1-58089-327-5 (softcover)
1. Troy (Extinct city)—Juvenile literature. 2. Trojan War—Juvenile literature. 3. Excavations (Archaeology)—Turkey—Troy (Extinct city)—Juvenile literature. 4. Greece—Civilization—To 146 B.C.—Juvenile literature. 5. Civilization, Mycenaean—Juvenile literature. 6. Archaeologists—Biography—Juvenile literature. I. Rubalcaba, Jill. II. Brannen, Sarah S. III. Title.
DF221.T8C53 2010
939'.21—dc22   2010007586

Printed in China
(hc) 10 9 8 7 6 5 4 3 2 1
(sc) 10 9 8 7 6 5 4 3 2 1

Illustrations done in watercolor and ink on Arches hot-press paper
Display type and text type set in Herculanum and Centaur MT
Color separations by Chroma Graphics, Singapore
Printed and bound September 2010 by Yangjiang Millenium Litho Ltd. in Yangjiang, Guangdong, China
Production supervision by Brian G. Walker
Designed by Diane M. Earley

TABLE OF CONTENTS

BULGARIA

BLACK

MACEDONIA

STRAITS OF
DARDANELLES

ALBANIA

Mt. Olympus

GREECE

AEGEAN SEA

Hisarlik (Troy)
Mt. Ida

TURKEY
(Ancient Anat

ITHACA

Athens •

Mycenae •

Sparta •

SEA OF CRETE

CRETE

MEDITERRANEAN SEA

LEGEND

GREECE

TURKEY

HISARLIK (TROY)

• CITY

(SHOWS MODERN-DAY BORDERS)

LIBYA

EGYPT

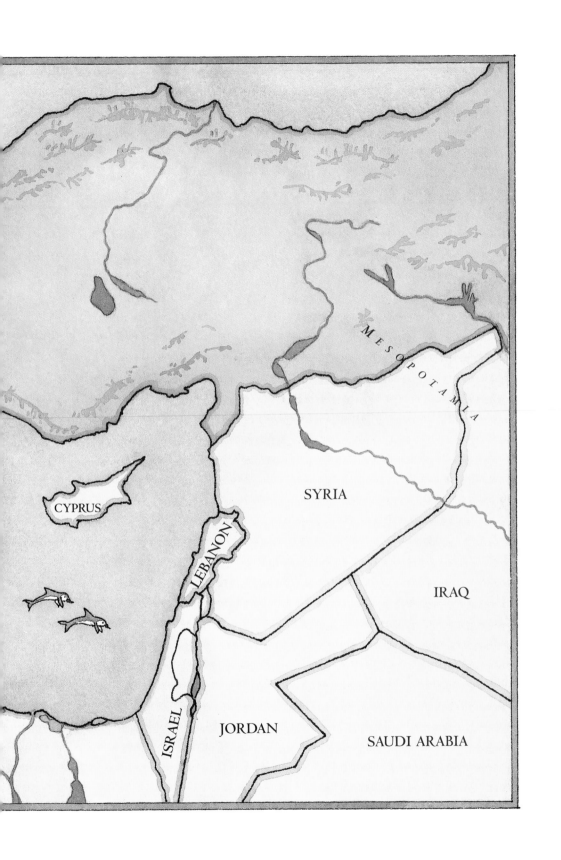

Close-up view of walls of Troy VI

INTRODUCTION

Hollywood's portrayals of archaeologists, such as the classic Indiana Jones, are about as close to the truth as Mickey Mouse is to a real mouse. Yet Hollywood may have gotten something right in their swashbuckling adventures. Sometimes the fantastical details of a legend really do stir adventurers into action. So it was with Homer's epic poems, *The Iliad* and *The Odyssey*, and entrepreneur Heinrich Schliemann. What better way to immortalize his name, Schliemann thought, than to discover the setting of the notorious Greek assault instigated by immortal gods? With that ambition he set in motion a search for Homeric Troy that would eventually span centuries and capture the imaginations (and ire) of scholars and the public alike.

Hisarlik, which means Place of Fortresses in Turkish, was the modern name given to the site where Schliemann believed Troy once stood. No larger than an American football field, it was overgrown and crumbling.

Located in Turkey near the Aegean Sea, it sat on a hill overlooking an expanse of flat land and the sea beyond. It was on this lookout in 1870 that Schliemann first sunk his spade in search of Homer's Troy. For the next two decades, Schliemann launched his own assaults on Troy, digging for (and often providing where there was none) proof of Homer's tales. After Schliemann, during the 1893 and 1894 digging seasons, archaeologist Wilhelm Dörpfeld attempted to sort out the jumble Schliemann had made of Hisarlik's layers. Dörpfeld was followed by American archaeologist Carl Blegen, who excavated the site between 1932 and 1938. Blegen took care to uncover the history of Hisarlik and the people who lived there. Half a century later, archaeologist Manfred Korfmann gave the world a new and controversial picture of Troy, not only by mapping Hisarlik using the latest technology, but also by establishing a museum and a national park at the site.

All of the archaeologists, professional and amateur, understood that the mound they were digging through was composed of many layers built up over time by human occupation after human occupation. There was no one Troy, but many versions spanning from 3000 BCE through the fall of the Roman Empire. Each archaeologist refined our understanding of the layers, which were labeled Troy I–IX, until those 9 phases were subdivided into 47 occupations, each formed by rebuilding after destruction, invasion, or abandonment. Could one of those 47 levels be the Troy that Homer wrote about? If so, which one?

Schliemann was certain he'd found Homer's legendary city in Troy II, but he had a hard time convincing anyone else. Schliemann's obsession to find evidence to prove a point he'd already made up his mind about did little to convince trained archaeologists that his approach was one of objective scientific enquiry. Dörpfeld suggested Troy VI as the candidate for Homer's Troy—he believed that Troy II was 1,000 years too early.

Although Blegen was a trained archaeologist, he came to Hisarlik in 1932 with the same conviction as the amateur Schliemann—that the Trojan War was historical fact. It was in Troy VIIa that Blegen found signs of a siege followed by a sacking that convinced him Homer's Troy had occurred at that level.

Recent excavations from 1988 to the present, led by Korfmann until his death in 2005, have been conducted by international teams of scholars. Korfmann's caution about taking a stand on whether or not there was a Trojan War is opposite to Schliemann's eagerness to do so. However, despite Korfmann's reluctance to speculate on the historical accuracy of Homer's story, he speculated on other things, such as the size of the city in layer VI. He also interpreted ditches at Hisarlik as lines of defense while his critics see them as irrigation trenches. It's hard to escape Homer's allure—even for the most objective scholar.

And then there's the Trojan Horse. Everyone, it seems, has a theory about that. Some suggest that the horse was really a siege tower, a common structure at the time the Trojan War was supposed to have been fought—sometime around 1250 BCE. Others suggest the horse was a metaphor for reinforcements arriving in the form of more Greek ships because Homer called ships "horses of the sea." And some scholars have theorized that it was a symbol for Poseidon, god of horses, earthquakes, and the sea. They claim that Homer was taking poetic license in describing a city whose final blow came by way of earthquake. The only theory not taken seriously is Homer's portrayal of a hollow horse hiding Greek soldiers.

Another element of Homer's epic that scholars don't take literally is the length of the Trojan War. Homer wrote that the Greeks fought for nine years and finally won in the tenth. During Homer's time the expression "nine times and then a tenth" meant lasting a very long time. Was Homer employing the expression to give a sense of time passing?

If the Trojan War did occur, it could have been lengthy, but it's unlikely to have lasted ten years.

So how did each archaeologist attempt to separate fact from fiction? Did the Trojan War really happen? And if it did, was it fought in the shadows of the stone walls of Hisarlik? Let's get digging and find out.

> . . . [S]leep, love, sweet song, and stately dance . . . these are things of which a man would surely have his fill rather than of battle.
>
> —*Homer*, The Iliad

Pronunciation Guide

These English-speaking pronunciation suggestions are not hard and fast rules. Spanish readers, for example, might pronounce many of these names quite differently. Even among English-speaking readers there are many accepted variations. These suggestions are some of the more common ways to pronounce the following Greek names.

Achilles uh-KILL-eez
Aeschylus ESS-kuh-luhs
Agamemnon ag-uh-MEM-nawn
Aphrodite af-roh-DYE-tee
Apollo a-PAWL-loh
Apollodorus a-pawl-loh-DOR-us
Artemis ART-uh-miss
Athena uh-THEE-nah
Atreus AY-tree-uhs
Aulis AWL-luhs
Boreas BOR-ee-uhs
Cassandra kuh-SAN-druh
Chryseis krye-SEE-uhs
Eris ERR-ihs
Euripides yur-IP-id-eez
Hector HEK-tur

Hecuba HEK-yoo-buh
Hera HIR-uh
Hisarlik HISS-ar-lik
Ilios ILL-ee-ohs
Iphigeneia if-uh-juh-NYE-uh
Menelaus men-uh-LAY-uhs
Mycenae my-SEE-nee
Odysseus oh-DIS-ee-uhs
Ovid AW-vid
Patroclus puh-TROH-klus
Peleus PEE-lee-uhs
Priam PREE-am
Styx STIKS
Thetis THEE-tis
Zeus ZOOS

THE LEGEND

Sing, O goddess, the anger of Achilles son of Peleus, that brought countless ills upon the Achaeans. Many a brave soul did it send hurrying down to Hades, and many a hero did it yield a prey to dogs and vultures, for so were the counsels of Jove fulfilled from the day on which the son of Atreus, king of men, and great Achilles, first fell out with one another.

—Homer, The Iliad

When your family gets together, do they retell old stories? Is there a story that you love (or hate) to hear again and again? Retelling old tales is how we preserve our personal histories.

Imagine a time before writing. Histories of entire countries were preserved in legend—no history books to recount the past, only the stories told aloud and handed down from generation to generation. Stories repeated about great loves and bloody battles, heroic deeds and treacherous betrayals—stories like the destruction of Troy.

Today we cobble together the tale of the Trojan War from the works of great playwrights and poets, storytellers and historians. A Greek living two thousand years ago would know all these bits and pieces from stories that had been spun for generations. We flesh out the tale from the poets Homer and Virgil, the playwrights Euripides and Aeschylus, and the prose writer Apollodorus, among others. Although there are slight differences, depending on who is telling the tale, the main plot holds fast.

Homer's *Iliad* recounts fifty-four days of heated battle in a poem about Ilios—one name for the city of Troy. Homer uses both Ilios and Troy interchangeably in his epic poem. What leads up to those fifty-four days of the Trojan War starts long before Homer's retelling. It begins with a prophecy. . . .

● ● ●

Hecuba, Queen of Troy, was pregnant again. Loving children, as good mothers—even queens—do, she eagerly awaited the time she would give her eldest son, Hector, a baby brother or sister. But this pregnancy was different. Hecuba's sleep was troubled. One night she dreamt that, instead of giving birth to King Priam's child, she bore a torch of flaming snakes. The sparks they spat caught in the tall grass, spreading wildly until the entire plain of Troy roiled with fire. In Hecuba's nightmare her home, the great walled city of Troy, smoldered in blackened ruin.

King Priam summoned the royal dream interpreters. What could this mean, this fiery end?

The soothsayers muttered among themselves, solemnly nodding in agreement. It could mean but one thing. The nightmare was a warning— the unborn child a curse. Troy was doomed.

"Unless."

"Unless?"

"Take the infant to the forest. Leave him there to die."

Heartbroken, Hecuba handed her newborn son to a servant.

King Priam barked orders to mask his own sorrow and guilt. "Take him deep into the forests of Mount Ida—to a place where no one will find him. Do it for the future of Troy."

The servant carried the bundled babe up the mountainside. He left the sleeping child in the open and hurried home before darkness fell.

A bear lumbering along, snacking on berries, grunted when it heard a plaintive cry. Nose tipped to the sky to catch the unfamiliar scent, the bear stood poised for a moment, then dropped to all fours and followed the sobs. The infant grasped the bear's fur in his fists. The bear snorted

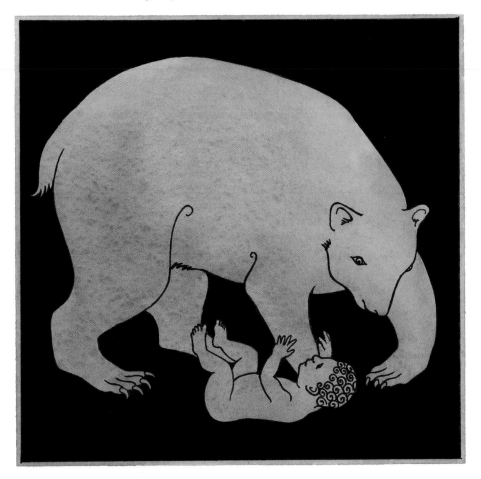

and then settled down beside the babe, providing warmth through the night. Five days the bear stood guard, and when on the fifth day it sniffed danger in the wind, it trundled off into the trees.

A herdsman calling for a missing calf broke through the underbrush, nearly stepping on the infant, who was waving his fur-coated fists in the air and gurgling.

The herdsman took the babe home to his wife, who named the boy Paris, and raised him as her own. Paris grew strong and extraordinarily handsome. He spent his days wandering the woods and pastures of Mount Ida unaware of his royal heritage and his own unmatched beauty.

While Paris tended his father's sheep, the gods of Mount Olympus celebrated the sea goddess Thetis's marriage. Everyone was invited. Everyone, that is, except the goddess of discord, Eris, who (for obvious reasons) was never invited to parties. In a foul mood Eris attended the wedding anyhow, determined to cause more trouble than usual.

Eris rolled a golden apple onto the banquet table. Written on the apple were the words "for the fairest." All the goddesses squabbled, each believing they were most deserving of that title. After a time the competitors narrowed to three—Hera, the goddess of marriage; Athena, the goddess of wisdom; and Aphrodite, the goddess of love.

Hera called on her husband Zeus to settle the dispute.

"Which one of us is the fairest? Who should get the apple?"

Zeus knew better than to choose. If he picked one, the other two would make his life miserable (particularly his wife Hera). So he wisely refused to judge. None of the other gods were fool enough to volunteer.

"The fairest mortal should be the one to pick the fairest immortal," Zeus proclaimed, secretly relieved by his own cleverness.

The three goddesses materialized on the hillside of Mount Ida directly in front of Paris and demanded he choose the fairest of them.

"If you choose me, I shall make you the wisest in all the world," Athena promised.

"Choose me, and wealth and power shall be yours," Hera promised.

Aphrodite stepped close to Paris and whispered in his ear, "The most beautiful woman in the world will love you and no other."

Paris handed Aphrodite the apple.

●　●　●

Every three years on the plains of Troy, King Priam held a festival. Paris had always been forbidden to go. His adopted father had good reason

for not wanting Paris to show himself in the city, but of course Paris knew nothing of this. Determined to enter this year's games, Paris snuck off to Troy without telling his father.

He entered three races, winning all three and angering the king's sons, who did not take losing well. They had drawn their swords and were ready to lop off Paris's head when an old shepherd pushed through the crowd yelling, "Stop!"

The shepherd, Paris's adopted father, trembled, sure that he would be severely punished for disobeying the king and allowing the prophesied destroyer of Troy to live. He fell to his knees before the king. "I beseech you, spare your son."

Priam had never forgiven himself for abandoning his son, and so he welcomed Paris with true joy in his heart. Hecuba took her son in her arms. Only Paris's sister, Cassandra, was wary.

"What of the omen?" she asked. But the gods had been wicked to Cassandra, granting her the gift of prophecy, and along with it the curse of never being believed.

No one listened.

Paris quickly adjusted to royal life. No sooner had he traded a bed under the stars for one inside the palace, than he sought the woman Aphrodite had promised. The fact that the most beautiful woman in the world was already married—and to the king of Sparta, no less—did not deter him.

Slyly, Paris arranged for his father, King Priam, to appoint him leader of a delegation heading to Sparta. The king and queen, overjoyed at Paris's return, denied him nothing. Only Cassandra spoke out against his mission.

"Don't let Paris go to Sparta. It will mean our doom."

No one listened.

So Priam wished his son that the gods be with him and outfitted him with Troy's finest ship. Aphrodite sent fair winds that carried Paris swiftly over the sea to Sparta where King Menelaus graciously welcomed him. Paris established himself into the king's good favor so effectively that the king treated him like his own son, unaware of the betrayal that was soon to come.

Just as Aphrodite had promised, Helen, the most beautiful woman in the world, fell deeply in love with Paris the moment she laid eyes on him. At first opportunity the two slipped away to Troy. Lovesick Helen deserted King Menelaus, her child, Sparta, and all that she knew for Paris.

Bewitched by Helen's beauty, the Trojans vowed never to let her go. Only Cassandra warned them of the destruction that would follow.

But, of course, no one listened.

When Menelaus discovered he had been deceived by the two people he loved and trusted most, he vowed to be avenged and immediately left to ask his powerful brother King Agamemnon of Mycenae for help. Agamemnon was no stranger to treachery. His ancestors had been poisoned with it. But by the power of Zeus, no brother of his would go unavenged as long as the mighty Agamemnon drew a breath.

Agamemnon sent word to all Greek princes, chieftains, and warriors, reminding them of the oath they took on Helen's wedding day. Each had sworn to defend Helen's chosen husband against any man bold enough to steal her away. That time had come. A thousand black ships and fifty times as many men set sail for Troy and vengeance.

●　　●　　●

Not every Greek was eager to chase after the faithless Helen. When Odysseus, the king of Ithaca, received his summons to join the attack against Troy, he consulted an oracle. The oracle prophesized that if Odysseus left for Troy, he would not return home for a very, very long time. True to his nickname—Odysseus the Cunning—Odysseus hatched a devious plot to release him from his vow to retrieve Helen.

When Odysseus's spies told him that Agamemnon's herald was near, Odysseus pretended he had gone stark raving mad. Like a crazed farmer he plowed the beaches, planting salt instead of seeds. With a donkey hitched next to an ox, their gaits unmatched, the plow lurched in all directions, adding to the madness. But the herald was not fooled by clever Odysseus, whose reputation for trickery was well known. Grabbing Odysseus's little boy, the herald tossed him directly in the plow's path. Odysseus turned the plow to avoid his son.

"Aha, your ruse is revealed," the herald called to Odysseus.

●   ●   ●

Thetis did not want her son, Achilles, to go to battle over Helen any more than Odysseus had wanted to fight. Although it had been her wedding the grievous golden apple had ruined, she did not seek revenge. She feared losing her beloved Achilles in battle far too much. Thetis sent Achilles disguised as a woman to a distant castle to hide among the maidens there. But an oracle had foretold that without Achilles there would be no taking of Troy, and so Agamemnon was determined to have him. If anyone could sniff out a scheme, it was Odysseus. So Agamemnon sent him in search of Achilles.

Disguised as a peddler, Odysseus arrived at the castle where Achilles hid. Gathering all the maidens around him, Odysseus threw open his trunk full of wares. The women admired the jewelry, fingered the fine cloth, and tapped the perfumes to their wrists. Only one maiden reached for a dagger. Odysseus snatched away the veil covering Achilles' face.

●   ●   ●

Odysseus and Achilles met the Greeks at Aulis. They prepared to set sail for Troy, but Boreas, the god of the North Wind, had other ideas for the black sails. He beat the ships back with tempestuous storms, and for days and then for weeks the Greeks were no closer to Troy than when they had begun. Agamemnon ordered his soothsayers to consult an oracle.

"Artemis, the goddess of hunting, is grieving. One of our countrymen has slain her beloved hare. She won't allow safe passage to Troy until you have sacrificed something you love equally well—your daughter, Iphigeneia."

At first Agamemnon refused. But soon his men's grumblings turned to talk of mutiny. So Agamemnon sent for his daughter under the pretense that she was to marry Achilles. When she arrived in her wedding dress, Agamemnon told her the truth. Through tears of shame he watched

his brave Iphigeneia walk to the altar and bare her throat to the execu-
tioner. The priest slit her throat with one powerful stroke. That night the
storm winds died, and the Greeks set sail for Troy.

●   ●   ●

Agamemnon offered King Priam one last chance to return Helen to
Menelaus. From his ship anchored in Troy's harbor, Agamemnon dis-
patched an envoy to appeal to Priam.

"Give up Helen, or give up Troy."

"Never!" the Trojans bellowed.

With this last attempt at peace failed, the Trojan War began.

The black ships beached on Trojan shores, and then the Greeks made camp.

The Trojans withdrew inside their great walled city, hunkering down for a long siege.

And long it was. For nine years the two stubborn enemies stood firm, neither keeping an advantage for long. The Greeks grew homesick, and the Trojans tired of their confinement, but neither side gave in.

Eris flitted about the Greek camps, delighted over the turbulence in the air. With patience worn thin from years without home or comfort, quarrels broke out over any slight. Eris was equally content inside the citadel. There tempers flared due to food gone bad and crowded housing.

The restless Greeks attacked and sacked towns up and down the coast. Plundered food filled their bellies, stolen treasures fed their greed, and kidnapped maidens made them forget their homesickness for a moment. Agamemnon took the choicest pickings for himself. Of the maidens, Chryseis, daughter of Apollo's priest, was the fairest.

Chryseis's father traveled to the Greek camp to beg for his daughter's release. He had brought more than enough gold to barter with, but Agamemnon abused the priest with insults and ordered him away. The priest left, but soon after he departed, the Greeks fell ill with a strange fever. One by one Agamemnon's men died, and the air grew thick with smoke from the death pyres.

Agamemnon summoned the soothsayer. "What evil plagues our camp?"

"You, sire. You have angered Apollo. You have insulted his priest. Apollo shoots plague-tipped arrows into our midst. Until you give up Chryseis, we will all suffer."

If Agamemnon was to give up Chryseis the Fair, he would have another. He sent two men to Achilles' tent to rob Achilles of his fairest slave.

Infuriated, the hot-tempered Achilles swore he'd never lift his sword in Agamemnon's defense. He'd sworn no oath to protect Menelaus. No oath promising to return Helen to Sparta. No oath to Greece. Achilles stormed off the battlefield, determined never to fight the Trojans again.

By now the gods in Olympus had all taken sides. Aphrodite stood firm with Paris, who had awarded her the apple. The rejected Hera and Athena stood just as firmly against him. Thetis, furious now at Agamemnon for the way he'd treated her son Achilles, appealed to Zeus to end the war—granting victory to King Priam and defeat to Agamemnon. Zeus was reluctant to take sides, knowing whoever he crossed would make his life disagreeable. But, in the end, Zeus gave in to Thetis.

Their plan was a simple one, especially for the gods, who tend to like intricate plots. That night Agamemnon would dream that victory against the Trojans was his if he attacked at daybreak.

The next morning Agamemnon awoke calling his men to arms. "We must march today. Zeus has guaranteed our success!"

The Greeks rushed the walled city.

The Trojans poured out of the gates.

The two armies brandished swords, screamed threats, and rushed to meet in battle. King Priam stood on the wall watching the mayhem below. The two armies pulled back, creating two lines facing one another. Between them stood Paris and Menelaus. It would be a fight to the death. Helen's lover against Helen's husband—with Helen as the victor's prize.

The first throw went to Paris. With raised shield Menelaus deflected the spear and then hurled his own with such force that the point shot clear through Paris's shield and breastplate. Paris felt the fabric of his tunic rip but not his skin. Bellowing with fury Menelaus drew his sword and crashed it down upon Paris's bronze helmet where the blade shattered into pieces. Now weaponless, Menelaus charged Paris, ready to fight barehanded. He grabbed Paris by his helmet and dragged him toward the Greek battle line. Alarmed that the fight would end with Paris administering but one blow, Aphrodite broke the helmet's strap, stirred up a cloud of smoke, and whisked Paris inside the great walls of Troy.

Agamemnon stepped forward. Paris had clearly lost the hand-to-hand combat. Both sides had witnessed Menelaus's courage and Paris's cowardice. "To the victor go the spoils! Bring Helen to the gate," Agamemnon demanded.

The Trojans were ready to hand over Helen when Hera and Athena interfered. The gods hold grudges, and they had not forgiven Paris for giving the apple to Aphrodite. They would not be satisfied until Troy lay in ruins.

Athena swept down onto the battlefield and whispered into a Trojan soldier's ear. "Shoot."

The arrow broke the uneasy truce, wounding Menelaus and enraging the Greeks. War!

The Greeks pushed the Trojans back, fighting boldly, shield against shield, sword against sword. When a man fell, his enemy tried to strip him of his armor and weapons while his countrymen stood over him, protecting him from the dishonor.

The fiercest Trojan of all, Hector—eldest son of Priam—drove his chariot through the Greeks like a man possessed. Greek after Greek died at the thrust of his spear—and under his courageous leadership, the Greeks were driven back to the sea.

That night inside Troy's great walls, the warriors celebrated. In the Greek seaside camp, the soldiers nursed their wounds. Even Agamemnon was losing hope. Only Achilles could beat Hector. And Achilles would not fight. Swallowing his pride Agamemnon offered Achilles whatever he wanted if only he would don his armor and lead the Greeks to victory against Hector. Achilles refused.

The next day Hector led the Trojans past the Greek's defensive line and to their ships.

Patroclus burst into Achilles' tent. "I beg of you, my dearest friend, give me your armor. I must rally our men. If you will not lead them, I must. It's our only hope now."

Achilles raised his cup—an offering to Zeus. "Grant Patroclus victory and bring my fellow warrior and closest companion back to me unharmed," he demanded.

The armor fooled the Trojans. One look at the invincible "Achilles" and the warriors scattered. Patroclus chased them to the Trojan wall where Hector turned to face him. Patroclus tried to step back into the protection of his men, but with his backward step Hector saw an opening and struck with force. His sword pierced Patroclus's belly. With that killing stroke, Hector felled Patroclus.

When Achilles heard of his beloved friend's death, he vowed revenge. The anger he'd fanned against Agamemnon now ignited into full rage against Hector. He would see Hector's death or his own. Nothing short of that would do.

The next morning, in a new set of armor fashioned by the gods, Achilles led the Greeks against the Trojans, killing hundreds with his spear. The Trojans fled back through the gates and inside the protective walls of Troy—all except Hector who, despite Priam's pleads to come inside, stood to face Achilles.

The two warriors circled one another. Hector hurled his spear with all his might. It bounced uselessly off Achilles' divine shield. Pulling his knife from a sheath that hung at his thigh, Hector charged. Achilles ran to meet him driven by his own savage hatred. Finding an opening in Hector's armor at the collarbone, Achilles threw his spear. It pierced Hector through the neck.

Still enraged by Patroclus's death, Achilles stripped Hector's corpse of armor and tied the bleeding body by the ankles to the back of his chariot. With the bite of his whip, Achilles drove the horses like demons riding around and around the walls of Troy. Broken and dispirited, Priam, Hecuba, and all of Troy turned away in grief.

Achilles drove his chariot back to the Greek camp with Hector still dragging behind. That night, covered in the cloak of dark, Priam stole into Achilles' tent, humbling himself to his enemy. To Achilles he offered Hector's weight in gold if he could but give his son a proper burial. Achilles, seeing Priam's grief as deep as his own, broke down, his anger now extinguished.

Achilles ordered his servants to wash Hector's body and dress it in the softest linen robe they could find so that Priam would not see his son's body bloodied and battered. For nine days, while the Trojans mourned and buried their prince, the two great armies declared a truce.

And then they resumed fighting.

Even without Hector to lead them, the Trojans fought a good battle and many strong Greek warriors fell. Achilles valiantly led the Greeks right up to the walls of Troy. It would have ended then and there, but Paris shot a poisoned arrow and the gods saw to it that the arrow flew

true. It struck Achilles in the heel. As a child, Achilles' mother, the goddess Thetis, had dipped his mortal body in the River Styx, making him invincible—all but the heel by which she held him.

The two great Greek warriors Odysseus and Ajax fought like demons to protect Achilles' body from capture. Warding off blows, they inched their way back to the safety of their camp, dragging Achilles' lifeless form between them.

Another truce was declared—another fallen warrior mourned.

The Greeks burned Achilles' body on a funeral pyre and placed his ashes in the same urn as his beloved friend Patroclus. Thetis, encircled by her sisters' arms, collapsed in sorrow and wept—her beloved son Achilles no more.

● ● ●

Agamemnon awarded Achilles' divine armor to Odysseus. Ajax, sure that it was he who had earned the armor with his bravery, fell into a jealous rage. He plotted to kill Agamemnon and Odysseus to restore his honor. But Athena, looking down from Olympus, feared that with so many leaders dead, the Greeks would lose and Aphrodite would have her way—again. So Athena cast madness upon Ajax.

Not in his right mind, Ajax declared war on the Greek flocks of sheep and goats. Convinced he was battling Trojans, Ajax swung his sword again and again throughout the night, until on day's break he looked over the plain to see it strewn with slaughtered animals, his body encrusted with their blood.

Shamed, Ajax plunged the hilt of his sword into the ground and threw himself upon the point.

With Achilles and now Ajax gone, the Greeks were despondent. There was but one last hope. Kill Paris. With Paris dead, the Greeks were convinced Helen would give up Troy and return home. But Paris was not much of a warrior. He was too cowardly for hand-to-hand combat. He preferred to face his enemies from a distance, and so he favored the bow and arrow. The Greeks arranged for a master archer to challenge Paris to a match that would draw him out from behind Troy's protective walls.

Paris managed to shoot first but missed, and the archer returned three arrows simultaneously. He wounded Paris in the ankle, hand, and eye. The Trojans carried Paris back inside the walls and to Helen.

Paris died in Helen's arms.

But still Helen did not come forth.

Desperate, the Greeks hatched one last plot.

The schemer Odysseus designed a huge hollow wooden horse. Carpenters cut a nearly invisible trapdoor into the horse's hindquarter. Odysseus perched a ladder against the opening and warned the warriors climbing inside not to make a sound until they were given the signal. The Greeks then pretended to strike camp, board their ships, and sail home. Once hidden on the far side of a nearby island, the fleet dropped sail and waited. One Greek soldier remained behind with the story Odysseus had made him memorize.

The next morning Trojan lookouts in the parapets could not believe what lay below. In front of the gates, an enormous wooden horse stood, and behind it the Greek camp appeared deserted, the harbor empty of Greek ships. The Greeks had given up!

Ten long years of warfare and siege were over. The Trojans flooded out of the gates cheering. One lone Greek staggered out of hiding. The Trojans dragged him to Priam where the Greek convincingly wept his way through the story Odysseus had taught him: Agamemnon intended to use him as a human sacrifice to appease the gods. But he had managed to escape into the swamp. He no longer wanted to be a Greek. He swore allegiance to Priam and all of Troy.

"But what of the monstrous horse?" the Trojans asked.

"An offering to Athena. Surely, something so grand would please her. And it's too large for you to bring into the city and steal the glory. Agamemnon hopes you will burn it where it stands and bring Athena's wrath down on your heads for destroying her tribute."

Cassandra warned Priam. "Beware Greeks bearing gifts."

But no one listened, as was her fate.

One other doubted the story. He begged Priam to be wary. But as he spoke, two vile serpents rose up out of the sea and wrapped their coils

around the man, dragging him to a watery grave. The Trojans, convinced the serpents were Athena's doing, shouted, "Bring in the carven image."

So the Trojans dragged the wooden horse through their gates and inside the city walls.

In the middle of the night, when all was quiet and the Trojans lay in a deep sleep, weary from their celebrations, the Greek warriors crept out of the belly of the horse. They threw open the gates of Troy for the Greek army that was waiting outside the walls.

Racing through the city, soldiers torched building after building until all of Troy was in flames. When the Trojans stumbled out of their doors, still groggy with sleep, the Greeks butchered them—men, women, children hacked down.

The sun rose on a city in ruin. Hecuba, once a queen, now a captive, looked over the smoldering city of her nightmare. Anguished, she wailed, "What sorrow is there that is not mine? Country lost and husband and children."

The Greeks led the few Trojan women who had survived the massacre aboard the black ships. Slaves now, they looked back at their once great city.

> . . . the city is given over to the flames, while the women and children are carried into captivity . . .
>
> —*Homer*, The Iliad

The fall of Troy—a prophecy fulfilled—and all because of an apple and a pretty face.

2 REMEMBERING SCHLIEMANN

My doom has come upon me; let me not then die ingloriously and without a struggle, but let me first do some great thing that shall be told among men hereafter.

—*Homer*, The Iliad

Important people are often remembered through their "papers"—diaries, journals, and letters. Schliemann wanted to be remembered. He saved notebooks, diplomas, newspaper clippings, bills, appointment cards, invitations, and letters—thousands of letters, 60,000 in all. Fearing that the people he wrote to might not have the foresight to save his letters, Schliemann made copies, a tricky task in the mid-1800s. He wrote in special, slow-drying ink and then pressed the page under a sheet of transparent paper. The tissue copy paper absorbed the ink, creating a blurry copy. One year Schliemann wrote 1,800 letters. Throughout his lifetime he filled many 500-page, tissue-paper copy books. Ever frugal, he used every square inch of each page.

Heinrich Schliemann, the successful businessman

Still, Schliemann worried. He worried that the details of his life weren't memorable enough to make the history books. True, he had experienced remarkable things in his life—he had survived a shipwreck, knocking out his two front teeth when the ship went down. He'd ridden an elephant in India, and he'd stood on the Great Wall of China. He'd mastered 22 languages. He'd made not one, but two fortunes—the first as an indigo merchant in Russia and the second trading gold during the California Gold Rush. But many people had done those things, and as far as Schliemann could tell, they probably wouldn't be remembered. To Schliemann the details of his life were far too ordinary. He wasn't terribly handsome. He suffered from chronic earaches. His high-pitched, nervous laugh had no sense of humor driving it. He would never make his mark as a statesman because he had no interest in politics. He barely noticed the Civil War bloodying America's South.

The now-divorced Schliemann decided that what he needed was another wife. This second time around, he figured he had learned exactly what qualities make the perfect wife. He wrote to a friend asking for help with the search. The woman he had in mind should be well-educated, but poor, ". . . with black hair and, if possible, beautiful. . . . But my main requirement is a good and loving heart." Most important, she must read Homer. Schliemann assured his friend that he could tell everything he needed to know from a picture. His friend sent several. Schliemann dismissed one after another—too bossy, too ill-tempered, too domineering (all this decided from the pictures alone). Finally, Schliemann settled on a student who was about to become a teacher. Her name was Sophia Engastromenos. Schliemann wrote his friend, "I swear she is the only woman who shall be my wife."

Schliemann left America to meet Sophia in Athens, Greece, where he told her, "If you marry me, it must be so that we can excavate together, and enjoy a common enthusiasm for Homer." She must have liked Homer, and maybe even Schliemann as well, because 19 days later they were married. Schliemann was 47, and Sophia just 17.

With the marriage business taken care of, Schliemann turned his attention to what else he wanted. And what Schliemann wanted most was to be remembered like the heroes in Homer's epic poem, *The Iliad*. He wanted people to speak his name centuries after his death. If he could find Troy—Homer's setting for *The Iliad*—that would be something no one would ever forget.

While most scholars thought Homer was simply a good storyteller, Schliemann believed that Homer was a historian. There were only a few people who thought that Troy was more than a myth. During the summer of 1868, it was Schliemann's good fortune to meet one of them, Frank Calvert, a British diplomat who in his spare time had been looking for Troy in Turkey. While Troy seekers busily dug in a village five miles away, Calvert's careful research and excavation had convinced him that Homer's Troy was at Hisarlik. The mound at Hisarlik dominated a plain in western Turkey near the entrance of a strait that connects the Aegean Sea to the Black Sea. Calvert had bought the land in hopes of one day having enough money to fund a full-scale excavation. When Schliemann came along—rich and ready—Calvert eagerly provided Schliemann with all his data.

A complete beginner, Schliemann peppered Calvert with endless questions: "Have I to take a tent and iron bedstead and pillow with me . . . ? For all the houses in the plain of Troy are infested with vermin. . . . What sort of hat is best against the scorching sun?" Calvert patiently replied to all of Schliemann's questions; be sure to bring tea, he said, and as for a hat, the Turks had the best design, a white muslin turban. Meanwhile, Schliemann made copies of his own letters—letters he wrote to friends about his discovery, with no mention at all of Frank Calvert.

The mound of Hisarlik raised from rebuilding settlement on top of settlement

While surveying the site for the first time in 1868, Schliemann wrote in his diary that he stood on the mound at Hisarlik overlooking the windswept plain below "with my flesh creeping and with goose-pimples covering my skin." He pictured "the handsome Paris and fair Helen landing at this spot in their flight from Sparta." He imagined the Trojans hauling on ropes, pulling the wooden horse inside their city walls. With a spade in one hand and *The Iliad* in the other, he claimed to have at last found the site of Homer's Troy.

Schliemann was no archaeologist. He was no scholar. He made a lot of mistakes. Convinced that Troy was at the very bottom of the mound at Hisarlik, at the onset of his first campaign in 1870 he armed his workmen with pickaxes and ordered a huge trench dug into the center of the mound. Frank Calvert urged him to dig several small, less destructive trenches. An archaeologist begged Schliemann to take careful notes of the depth and location of every find. Each layer, he told Schliemann, contained the remains of a different settlement, one built on top of another. Record what you find. Schliemann ignored them both.

Schliemann's methods were savage and brutal. He plowed through layers of soil and everything in them without proper record keeping—no mapping of finds, few descriptions of discoveries. Single-mindedly Schliemann chopped his way toward Troy. He pushed himself to exhaustion. The workday began at first light. They worked until the sun set and the light was too dim to continue. Schliemann oversaw it all, pacing the site with his odd gliding walk. Later, by lamplight, Schliemann wrote the events of the day in a plain, stiff-covered notebook. He recorded the number of workmen, the day's expenses, and the progress on the dig. Sometimes he sketched the objects they had found that day. Today, archaeologists wouldn't wait until the evening to write out their notes. They wouldn't rely on their memory, which is unreliable; they take notes right in the trench. But Schliemann was never concerned with accuracy. Particularly when the truth didn't fit the story he was spinning. Because he had decided the summit of the hill would be the logical place for the most impressive buildings to have stood, when he found walls elsewhere he merely moved them to the summit in his official reports.

Deeper and deeper Schliemann's crew dug. Their shovels struck fragments of pottery archaeologists call potsherds. The deeper they dug, the more mud brick they uncovered—ancient walls, zigzagging everywhere. Their pickaxes and shovels obliterated history. In his diary Schliemann wrote, "Unfortunately we are obliged to destroy the foundations of a building 59 feet long and 43 feet broad." If it wasn't Homer's Troy, he wasn't interested. At 30 feet they struck (and shattered) more pottery, tools, and weapons. But it wasn't Homer's Troy. Schliemann kept digging.

In 1872, when Schliemann returned from a brief respite from digging, he arrived at Hisarlik like a general leading an army to battle. He

hired a miner, a railroad engineer, and 125 workmen. He equipped them
with the best battering rams, pickaxes, wheelbarrows, and spades. He
paid every workman a bonus when they brought him a find and docked
their wages when they faked one. He built himself a house and a store-
room on the site so that he could be close by. Schliemann meticulously
recorded every penny spent. He worked like a man possessed. Hurricane
winds choked the workmen with dust and dirt. Owls and frogs kept the
men awake at night with their shrieks. "Marsh sickness" (which was
probably malaria) crippled the workforce. Those well enough to climb
into the trenches were plagued by scorpions dropping on them from
above. Poisonous snakes slithered in and out of the rocks, biting the
workmen. Schliemann was sure the site would have been unworkable if
the storks hadn't eaten most of the snakes.

The deeper the trench, the more dangerous it became. Not many
workmen escaped injury from falling stones. At one point six men were
buried in a cave-in. When they were pulled from the wreckage, no one
could believe that they hadn't been crushed. Miraculously, they escaped
with only scratches. Work went on. And then Schliemann's luck changed.
On June 18, 1872, Schliemann wrote in his diary, "I am among the ruins
of Homeric Troy!"

Schliemann's gaping trenches uncovered a web of walls in a series of
cities built one on top of the other. At a break in one wall, Schliemann
uncovered a gate and, behind it, the ruins of a building. Never one to
avoid jumping to a conclusion when it was grand enough, Schliemann
announced he had found King Priam's palace. And in one room of the
palace, Schliemann claimed to have unearthed parts of a soldier's helmet
(which turned out to be the pieces of a smashed bronze vase). It wasn't
the first time Schliemann had jumped to conclusions. He had identified
a shield (which turned out to be a pan with its handle broken off). But

vases and frying pans just weren't romantic enough to capture the world's attention—and Schliemann wanted the world watching him. At the end of the 1872 digging season, despite coming down with "marsh fever," Schliemann was in high spirits and already making plans for his next season at Hisarlik.

Schliemann spun dramatic stories about his search for Troy around Homer's battles and the heroes who had fought them. If he found a cup, then Achilles must have drunk from it; if he found an earring, then Helen must have worn it. But nothing would make Schliemann as truly unforgettable as what happened next. On May 31, 1873, Schliemann discovered treasure. In his official report Schliemann wrote, "I came across a large copper object of the most remarkable shape, which attracted my attention all the more as I thought I saw gold behind it. . . . I cut out the treasure with a large knife. It was impossible to do this without the most strenuous exertions and the most fearful risk to my life, for the large fortification-wall, which I had to undermine, threatened at every moment to fall down on me. But the sight of so many objects, each one of which is of inestimable value for science, made me foolhardy and I had no thought of danger. The removal of the treasure, however, would have been impossible without the help of my dear wife, who stood always ready to pack in her shawl and carry away the objects I cut out."

Schliemann found gold and silver cups and dishes, bronze weapons and tools, thousands of gold beads, and jewelry, which he claimed to be the Jewels of Helen—the whole lot he called the "Treasure of Priam." The objects Schliemann found were nested so close to one another, he decided they must have been in a wooden chest, the chest itself rotted long ago. Close by he found what he claimed was the key to the chest. Schliemann wove a fantastic story of King Priam's family grabbing valuables and tossing them into a chest as the Greeks streamed out of the wooden

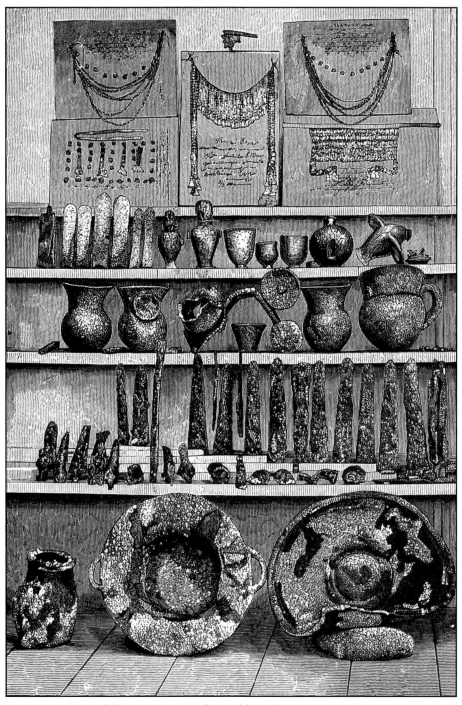

Lithograph of the so-called Treasure of Priam discovered by Schliemann

horse and fell upon Troy. With swords clanging all around them, there was no time to remove the key. The chest was heavy, laden with so many riches that the fleeing relative was forced to abandon his load when the enemy overtook him at the city wall. It was a dramatic imagining—too bad there wasn't any truth to it.

There are many problems with Schliemann's account—beginning with the date. Schliemann was fond of the idea that the "Treasure of Priam" was found in a room in the noble Trojan king's palace. It made the story more dramatic. But that room happened to be located under Schliemann's house. And his house was not moved for excavation purposes until June 3, three days after he discovered the treasure. It's also unlikely that Schliemann got down in the trench and risked being buried under a collapsing wall. If he had, then the Turkish overseer hired to watch Schliemann's every move would have become suspicious. Schliemann was probably far more concerned about the overseer demanding Turkey's fair share, half of the find, than rescuing valuables for science.

There are more holes in Schliemann's story of the "Treasure of Priam." Sophia, who supposedly helped him carry the treasure out of the trench in her shawl, was not even in Turkey at the time. According to Schliemann's own diaries, she was at home in Athens. The "key" that Schliemann found ended up being a chisel—which is not much of a surprise, considering keys had not yet been invented. Perhaps the biggest flaw in Schliemann's whole account was the fact that the "Treasure of Priam" dates to the Early Bronze Age, in the third millennium BCE. Even Schliemann himself was eventually forced to admit his error after finding Early Bronze Age pottery at excavations elsewhere that was similar to the pottery amid his so-called Treasure of Priam. Many historians now agree that if the Trojan War did indeed take place, it would have

Sophia Schliemann wearing gold jewelry from the "Treasure of Priam" found at Hisarlik

been in the 13th or 12th century BCE. The "Treasure of Priam" appears to be more than a thousand years older than Priam himself.

Some scholars even suggest that Schliemann staged the whole discovery. They claim that he hoarded finds as he excavated, waiting for the right moment to "discover" an unforgettable collection. It's certainly possible, given the lengths Schliemann was willing to go to so that he would be remembered. One thing is for sure, though—the man's hard to forget.

TROY'S NINE LIVES

I never recall my word, or deceive, or fail to do what I say, when I have nodded my head.

—*Homer*, The Iliad

Schliemann's escapade with the "Treasure of Priam" cost him his permission to dig in Turkey. The Turkish government did not take kindly to Schliemann's smuggling gold past their agent and out of the country. They revoked his permits. It would be two years before they would allow Schliemann back to Hisarlik, and four before he returned for a second campaign from 1878 to 1879.

Schliemann's third campaign at Hisarlik began on March 1, 1882. By now Schliemann realized that if he wanted to be taken seriously by the academic community, he could no longer behave like a looter with a smash-and-grab mentality. Tired of the constant stream of criticism from scientists for his theories about Troy and his excavation methods, Schliemann expanded his Troy-seeking team to include seasoned archaeologists.

The walls of the Bronze Age homes at Troy had been built from mud brick, the roofs from small trees bound together and covered with dirt and thatch. Flammable construction materials and open cooking fires have always been a recipe for disaster. Entire towns burn to the ground when sparks leap from one roof to the next. The Trojans never bothered to clear away the wreckage after a fire; they merely leveled the debris and built new homes over the ruins of the old.

The layering at Hisarlik was typical of the times. It wasn't just destruction from fires, earthquakes, and storms that contributed to the mound. Trash did its share. Rubbish removal is a modern convenience. Except in the most lavish of homes, floors were made by simply packing the dirt. When a homeowner had finished with something, he just dropped it on the floor or tossed it out the door—bones, broken dishes, spoiled food—litter was strewn everywhere. When it got to be too much—probably the smell and the vermin became intolerable—the Trojans covered the whole mess with another layer of dirt.

This method of spring cleaning had been repeated so many times that in some Trojan homes roofs had to be raised and doorways rebuilt. Archaeologists love these lousy housekeepers. Beneath the renewed floors they can find a record of human history. From discarded everyday objects, they are able to piece together a lifestyle. Hisarlik went through so many rebuildings and housecleanings that 50 feet of debris accumulated.

During the 1890 Christmas holidays, while Dörpfeld diligently recorded their discoveries from that season, Schliemann visited Naples. Bothered by an ear infection, Schliemann was on his way back to his hotel when he suffered a stroke and collapsed on the street. He died the next day, December 26, 1890, in a hospital in Naples.

After Schliemann's death Dörpfeld carried on at Hisarlik, his excavations financed by Sophia Schliemann. For two seasons Dörpfeld applied his slow and methodical efforts. He uncovered defensive walls, palatial homes, broad streets, and grand gates—a citadel not unlike the one described by Homer. Schliemann had believed that Troy II was the city in Homer's epic. But Dörpfeld remained unconvinced. He realized from the potsherds and other items found in Troy II that the level was too early to be Priam's Troy by a thousand years. Dörpfeld favored the timing of Troy VI.

After Dörpfeld's last two seasons it would be nearly 40 years before archaeologists returned to take a fresh look at Hisarlik. This time Carl Blegen, from the University of Cincinnati, searched for Homer's Troy. Blegen and Schliemann couldn't have been more dissimilar. Blegen was quiet and thoughtful, pausing before speaking to consider his response, and generous in crediting others for their contributions.

Blegen was even magnanimous enough to forgive Schliemann's reck-lessness at Hisarlik. He wrote, "Although there were some regrettable blun-ders, those criticisms are largely colored by a comparison with modern techniques of digging; but it is only fair to remember that before 1876 very few persons, if anyone, yet really knew how excavations should prop-erly be conducted. There was no science of archaeological investigation, and there was probably no other digger who was better than Schliemann in actual field work."

Although Dörpfeld had done an amazing job deciphering the jumble of occupations at Hisarlik, he was hampered by the limits of archae-ological technology at the time. When Blegen arrived at Hisarlik in 1932, techniques had advanced. One example of how archaeology had progressed was in the pots. By this time scholars understood that pot-tery goes in and out of fashion and that one can use pottery to date the levels, in part by looking at the pottery found at other sites where dates are known. Where Dörpfeld had lumped all Late Bronze Age pottery

American archaeologist Carl Blegen, who directed excavations at Hisarlik for the University of Cincinnati from 1932 to 1938

together, Blegen was able to match pots to precise periods in history. For instance, the Trojans imported Mycenaean pottery—a Greek pottery with distinctive styles that changed over time—a fact that helped Blegen determine accurate dates for some of Troy's levels.

Blegen assigned levels Troy I, II, III, IV, and V to the Early Bronze Age—a period of occupation that he estimated ran at least 1,000 years, maybe longer. During this Early Bronze Age period, Troy evolved at a slow and steady rate. Blegen observed no dramatic change in the Trojans' customs or way of life, which he would expect to see if they were invaded and conquered. Instead Blegen deduced that the divisions in each of the levels between Troy I and Troy V were the result of major catastrophes—fires, earthquakes, or violent storms.

If it had happened the way Homer portrayed in *The Iliad*, then Blegen would have found evidence of a conquest. He would have seen a dramatic cultural shift. Instead, Blegen wrote, "The reconstructed Troy seems to have been occupied by the same people, who followed the same way of life and clung to the same traditions as their immediate predecessors."

Troy I, c. 2900–2450 BCE, Early Bronze Age

The first people to settle Troy set the tone for those who followed. Their first civil project was the construction of a defensive wall. They were building a fortress—a citadel. The village's harbor and location on the straits of the Dardanelles provided trade opportunities. As the humble village of Troy I prospered and the population grew, the Trojans built bigger and better walls.

From what Blegen could uncover in Schliemann's gaping trench, there was no sign of overcrowding. The parallel walls of the houses indicated neatly arranged freestanding single-room homes. As was the custom for people at the time, the bodies of infants were buried just beneath the floor. Archaeologists found one tiny skeleton in a shallow pit covered by a flat stone, and another buried in a pottery urn.

Although the centermost part of Troy I could not be excavated because of the buildings from Troy II that were above it, Blegen deduced that this was where Troy's ruler would have lived—until disaster struck. Fire reduced Troy I to rubble.

Troy II, c. 2450–2200 BCE, Early Bronze Age

The Trojans built Troy II in a circular design. The defensive wall surrounding the city was massive, with guard towers every 30 feet. The largest towers protected the main gates, opening west and south. Entering and exiting required passing under these towers through long corridors. This was not the modest settlement of Troy I, but the beginnings of the great Bronze Age city Homer described.

The richness of the Trojans' possessions suggested to Blegen a life of luxury—court ladies bedecked in jewels and royal guards armed with swords fashioned with lion-headed hilts carved from crystal. He found goblets and dishes hammered from silver and looms for weaving soft fabrics. Bones from lamb, goat, pig, rabbit, and deer, along with lentils and grain lying around in large heaps indicated that no one went hungry.

The good fortune of Troy II came to an abrupt end. The abundance of ash and charred debris, which had led Schliemann to believe this was the Troy in Homer's epic, testified to a catastrophic fire. Homeowners had no warning. They fled, leaving precious belongings behind. Amid the blackened ruins in nearly every house, archaeologists found valuables that the inhabitants would never have abandoned unless they had been given no choice.

Troy III–V, c. 2200–1700 BCE, Early Bronze Age to Middle Bronze Age

Although Dörpfeld called Troy III to Troy V "miserable villages,"

Blegen's excavation revealed a steady growth in Troy's population and size. Freestanding houses gave way to apartments with shared walls separated by winding lanes.

To archaeologists' great dismay, however, the residents of Troy V took to housekeeping, sweeping away the day-to-day accumulation of trash. Troy V, like its predecessors III and IV, was destroyed, as were all the other layers, by invaders, fire, or earthquake. But unlike III and IV, the end of Troy V marked the end of a long, unbroken, cultural line. A new Troy was to follow.

Troy VI a–h, c. 1700–1250 BCE, Middle Bronze Age to Late Bronze Age

Troy VI began in the middle of the Bronze Age and lasted so long that Blegen detected 8 distinct phases within it (a–h). Blegen observed many

The walls of Troy VI

innovations in building techniques and many differences in building styles between this version of Troy and the last. The defensive wall showed advances not only in masonry and engineering, but in design as well. The newcomers at Troy built an observation tower that overlooked the city and the plain beyond it. The tower protected a well that lay inside the fortress. In times of trouble, fresh water would always be available without citizens having to venture outside the protection of the massive wall surrounding the city.

Even the gateways were planned with defense in mind. Long narrow passageways forced enemies into a vulnerable position, open to attack from the top of the walls and from the inside of the fortress. No formidable charge was possible while squeezing through these corridors. The enemy could easily be picked off by archers or swordsmen.

This version of Troy was unlike anything that had preceded it. Blegen wrote, "The changes seem to me to be so unheralded, so widespread, and so far-reaching that they can only be explained as indicating a break with the past, and the arrival and establishment on site of a new people endowed with a heritage of its own."

It was in Troy VI that horses first appeared. No horse bones had been found in earlier layers. Perhaps the newcomers arrived on horseback.

Even the pots in Troy VI were different than what the Trojans had made in the past. Blegen found 98 new varieties of shape and design. Household crockery had suddenly changed radically—more evidence pointing toward a complete cultural upheaval.

Following potsherds, Blegen found the first and only cemetery associated with Troy to date. Buried just beneath the surface he found urns containing the cremated remains of adults and children.

Troy VI ended in total ruin. A destructive force toppled the massive defensive wall. Damage to the citadel was so catastrophic that Blegen believed the end must have been caused by earthquake. Within the ruins he found no human victims, so he speculated rumblings warned the Trojans, who were able to escape with their lives.

Troy VIIa, c. 1250–1175 BCE, Late Bronze Age

Dörpfeld divided Troy VII into two distinctive layers, labeling them Troy VIIa and Troy VIIb. Troy VIIa lasted only one generation, from 1250–1175 BCE. It was a time of hasty rebuilding. Their fortifications were sturdy enough, but no time was put into making them attractive. The spacious homes Blegen had found in Troy VI were replaced with miserable accommodations—small houses crowded together, sharing common walls.

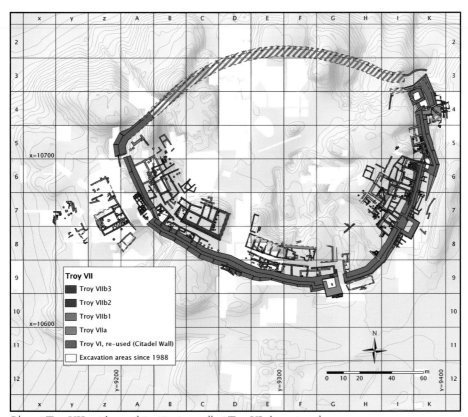

Plan of Troy VII, with reused fortification wall of Troy VI shown in red

A row of lean-to apartments built against the defensive wall housed some 20 to 30 units. What scared the Trojans into working so quickly?

Unlike Troy VI, Troy VIIa's end was no natural disaster. It was the result of human violence. Charred debris, blackened stone, and burned brick littered the streets and piled up over the ravaged houses. Archaeologists found skull fragments, a crushed cranium, a torn jawbone, and a skeleton that Blegen described as a body struck down and left to die where it fell.

The compilation of evidence convinced Blegen that Troy VIIa ended with a battle. He interpreted the crowded shantytown-style construction as an attempt to make room for everyone inside the city walls. The large storage jars found sunk into the floors in every home he construed as evidence of stockpiling supplies to last the duration of a siege. Blegen concluded that if the Trojan War had occurred as Homer had described, it was here, in Troy VIIa, that the Trojans faced the Greeks.

Blegen and his work were well-respected by his colleagues. His fastidious methods and detailed record-keeping were admired. The few critics who spoke out against Blegen's theories did not find fault with his excavating techniques. Instead they pointed out that much of the basis for choosing Troy VIIa as Homer's Troy was speculation. Where was the definitive proof?

Troy VIIb, c. 1175–1100 BCE, Late Bronze Age

Blegen believed that once the enemy retreated, and it was safe to return, the Trojans rebuilt their citadel. New houses rose up on the footprints of the old. Blegen believed that nothing had changed, except, perhaps, that the population was now tired and poor. And then, as history tends to do, it repeated itself. Troy was again captured, sacked, looted, and torched. This time the Trojans had had enough. They did not rebuild. For the next four centuries Troy sat on the hill—a ghost town.

Troy VIII, c. 700–85 BCE, Greek Period

Eventually the Greeks rebuilt the abandoned Troy. According to literature from that period, Troy became a holy place, a shrine to Athena. Many buildings were constructed during the Greek Period, including a temple to Athena, a town hall, and a theater.

Troy, now a sleepy Greek village, witnessed the ebb and flow of history as tyrants rose and fell in the Greek world. Democracy was invented, the Persians tried to invade Greece and were defeated, and then Alexander the Great came through on his triumphant campaign, traveling out of his way to Troy in 334 BCE to make sacrifices to Athena en route. Some ancient historians claim Athena's priests gave Achilles' own shield and weapons to Alexander and that from then on he carried these in his own conquests.

In 85 BCE, Troy was once again thrown into upheaval and destroyed violently.

Troy IX, c. 48 BCE–550 CE, Roman Period

The Romans called Troy "sacred Ilium." To them Troy was the mother city of Rome. Under Julius and Augustus Caesar, Troy's temples were rebuilt and enlarged. Massive public buildings seating 6,000 were erected for musical and theatrical performances, the simple packed-dirt floors now covered in intricate mosaics. Roman baths, temples, grand civic buildings—all towered over the lower town, resurrected according to Roman design—a gridiron pattern. Roman engineers dug aqueducts. Water was piped into the city from the foothills of Mount Ida.

But the harbor was silting up. With Troy's strategic position in jeopardy, it began to decline. It was no longer the economic center it had once been. Troy had outlived the last of its nine lives. This final end would not be from enemy hand, or nature's forces. Abandoned, time toppled the city.

A Roman theater from the Roman occupation during Troy IX

Today the ruins are a national park. Hints of past grandeur remain in short stretches of walls sturdy enough to have survived the millennia. Paved ramps lead to forgotten gateways. The view over the open plain is still inspiring. One can imagine Priam looking out over his kingdom— hear the clash of swords, smell the acrid flames, feel the sorrow at the fall of Troy.

I too shall lie [down] when I am dead . . . Till then I will win fame.

—*Homer,* The Iliad

THE BIGGER THEY ARE, THE HARDER THEY FALL

Mighty was the uproar as the two forces met . . . the terrible shout which the Trojans and Achaeans raised as they sprang upon one another. Hector first aimed his spear at Ajax, who was turned full towards him, nor did he miss his aim. The spear struck him where two bands passed over his chest— the band of his shield and that of his silver-studded sword . . .

—Homer, The Iliad

Have you ever had trouble finding something? When you lose your house keys, you begin the search by looking in all the obvious places— your backpack, your coat pocket, the lock. Then, in desperation, you look in the not-so-obvious spots—the hamper, the refrigerator, the kitty litter box. It's often when you stop searching that you find your house keys. That's how things turned out at Hisarlik. It wasn't until archaeologists stopped looking for Homer's Troy that they found it.

When archaeologist Manfred Korfmann arrived at Hisarlik in the 1980s, he made it clear that he was not there to look for Homer's Troy. Korfmann wrote, "Despite assumptions to the contrary, archaeological

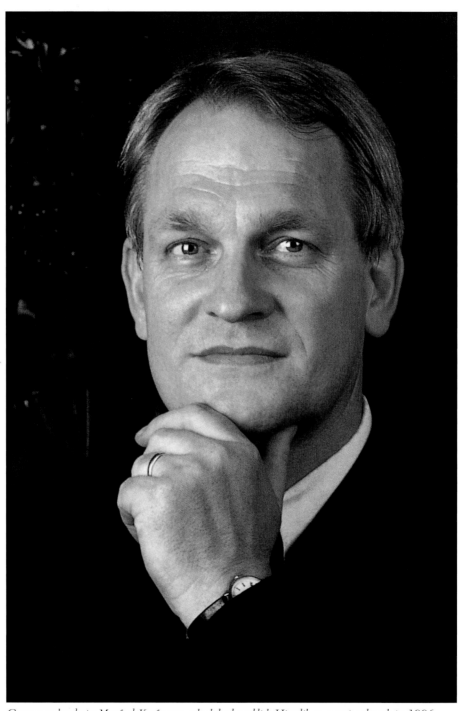

German archaeologist Manfred Korfmann, who helped establish Hisarlik as a national park in 1996

work of the new Troy project has not been performed for the purpose of understanding Homer's *Iliad* or the Trojan War." His interest in Hisarlik embraced the entire occupation—from its Early Bronze Age origins to its Roman decline and fall. It was not limited to one decade of bloody battle that many believed was a complete fiction. Korfmann approached Troy intending to study the entire settlement and its place as a hub of foreign trade, not as a subject of myth and legend. But what Korfmann ended up uncovering had scholars abuzz all over again about the Trojan War—fact or fiction?

Tremendous advances in archaeology had taken place between the time Blegen excavated Hisarlik in the 1930s and the time Korfmann excavated, but one new tool stood out above the rest—the magnetometer. This instrument "sees" underground much like an X-ray sees inside a human body. By reading the earth's magnetic field, the magnetometer can map what lies beneath the surface without having to disturb the site. Archaeologists then may choose to excavate small test sites to confirm and expand upon the picture. By using the magnetometer at Hisarlik, Korfmann discovered a city surrounding Troy VI's citadel—a city that would transform scholarly opinions about Troy.

Until Korfmann discovered the city outside Troy's walls, scholars wishing to discredit findings from earlier excavations claimed Troy was never more than a "nest of brigands and pirates" not worthy of invading. Even Blegen had described some of the Bronze Age levels as "wretched." But the magnetometer revealed a picture that even Troy's most cynical academic opponents were forced to accept. Troy VI was far from the impoverished outpost the skeptics had wanted to believe. The urban design boasted wide city streets lined with curbstones, public facilities such as theaters and baths, and a state-of-the-art water system that piped fresh water in and sewage out.

Korfmann's workers re-excavating Schliemann's original trench at Troy

The first clue that a city existed outside the citadel cropped up when the magnetometer showed archaeologists an image of a wall south of Troy VI's citadel. Korfmann planned test excavations for the following season to confirm the images. What he uncovered startled all 70 scientists working at Hisarlik. There was no wall at all. Instead they found a ditch.

The U-shaped ditch had been cut cleanly into the bedrock. It measured 10 feet wide and 8 feet deep. The magnetometer had "seen" the debris that filled the ditch, and scientists had interpreted those images as a wall. Korfmann surmised that during Troy VI the Trojans had dug a defensive ditch around the perimeter of their city to keep enemy chariots a bow shot away.

Further magnetometer readings revealed a break in the ditch. Clearly, Korfmann thought, this break in the ditch had served as an entrance ramp. The 30-foot-wide causeway bridged the ditch to allow carts, animals, and humans in and out of the city. In the middle of the causeway, Korfmann discovered post holes—footings for a wooden gate. Korfmann wrote, "In this way the passage of enemy chariots, for example, could be prevented, and access to the lower town and citadel of Troy controlled."

Near the gate archaeologists discovered a pile of mud bricks, which explained why a defensive wall had not been found. Over time mud bricks crumble and disintegrate. A wall had been there after all.

Another summer, another three-month digging season—and another ditch! Dating indicated that the second ditch, 300 feet outside the first ditch, had been dug after the first. Did the Trojans feel the need for a second

Photograph of Troy with overlay "pictures" taken by the magnetometer, showing unexcavated remains lying beneath the surface

line of defense? Something to keep battering rams and catapults at bay? Or had Troy VI grown to the point that living conditions inside the first ditch felt cramped and they needed more room to spread out? Either way, Troy's inner city was now well protected with two ditches and a wall.

Korfmann's discovery of the lower city painted a very Homeric picture of Troy VI/VIIa. The citadel appeared to have been a knight's castle overlooking its domain—a substantial city below, and a harbor beyond. Blegen's Troy VI covered 5 acres. Korfmann and the magnetometer revealed a Troy VI that was at least ten times bigger.

Size wasn't the only discrepancy with past perceptions of Troy VI. Apart from Mycenaean pottery, which was obviously imported from Greece, Korfmann was having a hard time seeing Greek influences in the city planning and architecture, unlike previous archaeologists who had worked at the site. Korfmann thought many of Troy's features were looking more Eastern than Western, resembling towns in Anatolia—the vast area between the Black and Mediterranean Seas now part of modern-day Turkey. The Greeks didn't dig defensive ditches, but Anatolians did. The Greeks rarely used mud bricks to build fortification walls, but it was a standard building material for the Anatolians. And the watchtowers spaced at intervals in the wall surrounding the citadel was a common feature in fortified walls in Anatolia.

Scholars call the people who lived in Anatolia at the time of Troy VI Hittites. The Hittites had a lot in common with the Trojans of Troy VI. They drank from the same style cups and mugs, ate from the same style plates and bowls, and poured from the same style pitchers. They shared a common technique for making pottery.

The Hittites believed that gods and spirits lived inside large stones. To protect their homes, streets, cemeteries, buildings, and towns, the Hittites placed human-sized stones decorated with carvings alongside entrances. Archaeologists call these stones stelae. More than a dozen stelae have been found at Troy beside the town's gates.

Inside one home in the Troy VIIa level, Korfmann found a stone pedestal tucked into the corner of one room. A bronze sculpture of an Anatolian god lay on the floor in front of the pedestal from which it had obviously fallen. The Trojans from this level had worshiped Anatolian gods.

As if all that wasn't enough evidence to link the Trojans with the Hittites and Troy VI with Anatolia, Korfmann found more support for the connection in a cemetery. Instead of practicing Greek burial rituals, the Trojans cremated their dead, placed the ashes in urns, and stored the urns in house-shaped tombs—all Hittite funerary customs.

Little doubt remained for Korfmann that Troy and Anatolia were connected during the second millennium BCE (especially during the time of Troy VI and VII)—and not just through trade, but through tradition. He wrote, "We know today, from our own excavations and even from earlier ones, that in all main respects, Bronze Age Troy had stronger ties with Anatolia than with the Aegean."

Troy's harbor made the town a valuable trading center. During the summer months strong northeasterly winds blustered through the nearby shipping lanes in the straits of Dardanelles, challenging the sails. In the days before sailors knew how to tack, or zigzag back and forth in order to make headway, sailing against the wind was impossible. To make matters worse, the powerful currents in the straits rendered oars useless. Ships were forced to wait out the contrary weather in Troy's harbor.

The winds could blow for days, weeks, sometimes even months, during which time shipmates would need food and water, with their ship's holds full of goods to trade for it. Troy's position as guardian of the harbor would have been a profitable one.

In the ancient world incoming ships were cause for great excitement. Exotic items from faraway places in Asia and Europe might be tucked away in the belly of the ship, or perhaps the captain brought along some curious foreign invention to be pulled out and mulled over. The Trojans took a fancy to the potter's wheel from Mesopotamia. The spinning surface revolutionized pot making—and Troy was the first Western region to import the device.

Although Troy served primarily as a middleman in the trading game because of its fortuitous location, the Trojans did have one unique good to sell. They had horses—fabulous horses.

In the second millennium BCE, the elite mode of transportation for warriors, hunters, and royals was the chariot. Chariots needed horsepower. The Hittites valued their horses above any other possession. Their manuals on the care and training of horses have survived the millennia. Surely, the Hittite obsession with horses would have created a strong demand. Did Troy supply it? By the sheer volume of horse bones present at Troy VI and VII, archaeologists speculate that Troy may have been a horse breeding and training center.

Archaeologists have discovered further proof of active maritime trade during the second millennium BCE along the east coast of the Mediterranean. Just as it is today, water transport was cheaper and faster than over land. For long-distance trade it was the most profitable route. Underwater archaeologists George Bass and Cemal Pulak discovered a shipwreck, dating back to 1300 BCE, off the coast of southwest Turkey, not all that far from Troy. Dazzled by the treasure of copper ingots—enough to manufacture 11 tons of bronze—Pulak speculated what this underwater treasure meant in terms of the breadth of trade in the second millennium BCE, "This gives us a clear idea of how intricate and how far reaching the ancient trade network is, it's much, much more sophisticated than we originally thought."

Underwater archaeologist examining the wooden keel and a stone anchor from the shipwreck

Troy's prime location along the sea-lanes ensured that as sea traffic increased, so did Troy's standing in the ancient world. Korfmann said in a BBC documentary, "The straits . . . are so narrow here that everything you could expect of contact between Asia and Europe should have passed here. So Troy could have benefited from this special geographic situation, and I think that's why it is so big in comparison to other sites."

From all the evidence unearthed at Hisarlik, Korfmann organized a museum exhibit entitled "Troy—Dream and Reality." *Archaeology* magazine described the exhibit as transforming "our understanding of ancient Troy from a legendary land of gods and heroes to a critical trading center of the Hittite Empire."

The exhibit's main attraction was a detailed wooden model of how Korfmann imagined Troy VI appeared 3,000 years ago—the citadel with its massive wall, towers, and gates, and the town below with grand housing for 10,000 residents. Not everyone shared Korfmann's vision. One particularly vocal scholar was a professor of ancient history from Korfmann's university, Dr. Frank Kolb.

Kolb attacked Korfmann publicly, calling the model a fiction and Korfmann a quack. "Pure fantasy. An archaeological Disneyland," Kolb accused. "This model was presented as a 'reconstruction,' although for more than 95 percent of its buildings there exists no archaeological evidence."

A new Trojan War ignited—scholars against scholars. Korfmann led one camp: "in this area there is no site as important as Troy." Kolb led the other: "to portray Troy as a center of trade and as a capital is a completely absurd scenario."

Determined to put an end to the bickering, the rector of the University of Tübingen in Germany where Korfmann and Kolb taught arranged a public debate. The two men stood before a standing-room-only crowd and exchanged barbs for more than three hours. The dispute ended in a stalemate, with neither side budging. Korfmann defended his interpretation of Troy as a significant site. Kolb accused Korfmann of distorting the evidence to support a vision of Troy as a great city. Kolb insisted there was no evidence at all to suggest that Troy was a major anything—too few artifacts to indicate a major trading center, too few foundations to indicate a major settlement outside the city walls. He insisted instead that the area was largely farmland. Kolb criticized Korfmann's exhibition model. According to him, it "falsely shows solid houses" where the excavation uncovered "only scattered wood and clay buildings and much free space."

Yet most archaeologists side with Korfmann. They point to the evidence emerging at Hisarlik—and to collaborating evidence elsewhere in the world. Korfmann points out, "Research by Anatolian specialists has shown that what we call Troy was in the Late Bronze Age the [Anatolian]

Revised artist's conception of Troy VI, with Korfmann's new evidence included

kingdom of Wilusa, powerful enough to conclude treaties with the Hittite Empire; even the Egyptians seem to have been familiar with the city. Furthermore, according to Hittite records, there were political and military tensions around Troy precisely during the 13th and early 12th centuries BC—the supposed time of Homer's Trojan War."

So what about it—was there a Trojan War? Was Troy important enough for the Greeks to launch a thousand ships and wage war over?

Many battles played out at Troy—the citadel's fortifications withstood repeated attacks. The defensive walls were rebuilt again and again.

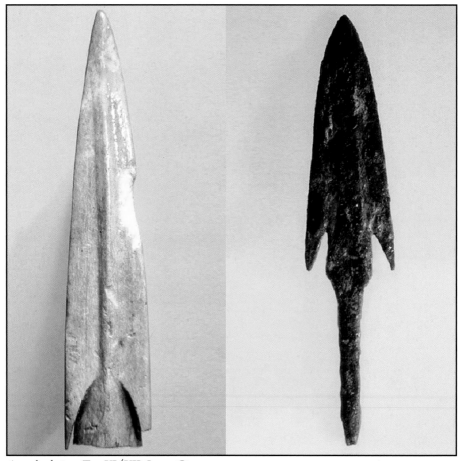

Arrowheads from Troy VI/VII, Lower City

Modern dating techniques indicate that Troy II—the settlement that Schliemann believed to be involved in the Trojan War—is more than 1,000 years too early to be Homer's war. By the same token Blegen's choice of Troy VIIa looks as if it is a bit too late to have been part of the war. Troy VI's timing, size, and standing in the ancient world, however, may be just right.

Today scholars generally agree that the evidence for Homer's Trojan War lies in Troy VI. (Although some still hedge their bets and call this level Troy VI/VII.) There are skeletons—one of a young girl, sixteen or seventeen years old—that suggest there was violence during this period. Archaeologists found her half buried, her feet burned by a fire. There were also sling pellets—heaps of them abandoned by the Trojans as they fled. A war inside the city was fought and lost. But was it Homer's Trojan

Slingstones from Troy VI/VII, Lower City

War? Korfmann, in all likelihood tired of being forced to defend a position he felt was substantiated, argued, "In light of the remarkable amount of discovery that has taken place over the last ten to fifteen years, the onus to defend positions should now be on those who believe there is absolutely no historical association between what happened at Late Bronze Age Troy and the events in *The Iliad*."

Korfmann died on August 11, 2005. But the search for Homer's Troy did not die with him. The story of lovesick Paris and the woman beautiful enough to launch a thousand ships continues to capture the imaginations of adventurous scholars. As Korfmann put it when asked if the battlements of Hisarlik once withstood Agamemnon's attack—"Why not?"

Conclusion

Archaeology, like all the sciences, is advancing so fast it's a challenge to keep up with new developments. Schliemann's attack on Hisarlik looks positively barbaric by today's standards. But as Blegen pointed out, there were no guidelines for excavations in Schliemann's time—to compare it to modern methods is as unfair as making comparisons in any other science. Medicine in the 19th century had still not caught on to the idea of contagion, and so surgeons went from patient to patient without bothering to wash the blood from their hands. Barbaric? Certainly. Which leads one to wonder how today's scientific methods will be viewed a century from now.

The story of Hisarlik and its many Troys and the story of the study of Hisarlik are entwined. Just as Troy has many stages, so do the excavations. From crude beginnings to cautious digging and meticulous record keeping to noninvasive modern techniques, Troy's investigation encompasses the history of archaeology itself. With each archaeological step forward, not only in method, but also in how archaeologists view their role, our picture of the past grows more complete. And with this higher definition we begin to separate fact from fiction within ancient literature. We may never know what caused the violent end of Troy VI—a pretty face or a struggle to overtake a lucrative hub of trade—but we do know more about how these ancient people lived in each settlement, what gods they may have worshipped, and how they defended their city over the years.

Yet, even stripped and laid bare by science with all its advancements applied, these old stories will always capture some adventurer's imagination and inspire a quest. For as Homer wrote, "And what he greatly thought, he nobly dared."

Troy's Timeline

2900–2450 BCE	Troy I (Early Bronze Age)*
2450–2200 BCE	Troy II (Early Bronze Age)
2200–1700 BCE	Troy III–V (Early Bronze Age to Middle Bronze Age)
1700–1250 BCE	Troy VI (Middle Bronze Age to Late Bronze Age)
1200 BCE	Trojan War (plus or minus 75 years)
1250–1175 BCE	Troy VIIa (Late Bronze Age)
1175–1100 BCE	Troy VIIb (Late Bronze Age)
750 BCE	Approximate birth date for the poet Homer, who is often credited as the author of the epic poems *The Iliad* and *The Odyssey*
700–85 BCE	Troy VIII (Greek Period)
334 BCE	Alexander the Great makes pilgrimage to Troy
48 BCE–550 CE	Troy IX (Roman Period)
1870–1890	Heinrich Schliemann excavates at Hisarlik (off and on)
1893–1894	Wilhelm Dörpfeld excavates at Hisarlik
1932–1938	Carl Blegen excavates at Hisarlik
1988–2005	Manfred Korfmann excavates at Hisarlik

*Note: All level dates are approximate.

BIBLIOGRAPHY

Acar, Ozgen. "At the Museums: Dream to Reality," *Archaeology* 54, no. 4 (July/August 2001), http://www.archaeology.org/0107/abstracts/museum.html.

Allen, Susan Heuck. *Finding the Walls of Troy: Frank Calvert and Heinrich Schliemann at Hisarlik.* Berkeley and Los Angeles: University of California Press, 1999.

———. "In Schliemann's Shadow: Frank Calvert, the Unheralded Discoverer of Troy." *Archaeology* 48, no. 3 (1995): pp. 50–57.

———. "Priam's Treasure in Boston?" *Archaeology Odyssey* 2, no. 3 (July/August 1999): pp. 28–29, 60.

Blegen, C. W. *Troy and the Trojans.* London: Thames and Hudson, 1963.

Brandau, Birgit. "Can Archaeology Discover Homer's Troy?" *Archaeology Odyssey* Premiere Issue (1998): pp. 14–25.

Bryce, Trevor R. *The Trojans and Their Neighbours.* New York: Routledge, 2006.

———. "The Trojan War: Is There Truth Behind the Legend." *Near Eastern Archaeology* 65, no. 3 (2002): 182–195.

Butler, Samuel. *The Iliad of Homer.* New York: Longman's, Green, 1898.

Calder III, William M., and David A. Traill. *Myth, Scandal and History.* Detroit: Wayne State University Press, 1986.

Dörpfeld, Wilhelm. *Troja und Ilion.* Athens, Greece: Beck & Barth, 1902.

Easton, Donald F. "Priam's Gold: The Full Story." *Anatolian Studies* 44 (1994): pp. 221–243.

———. "Schliemann's Discovery of 'Priam's Treasure': Two Enigmas." *Antiquity* 55 (1981): pp. 179–183.

———. "Schliemann's Mendacity—A False Trail?" *Antiquity* 58 (1984): pp. 197–204.

Finley, M. I. *The World of Odysseus.* New York: New York Review of Books, 1982.

Goldmann, Klaus. "Who Owns Priam's Treasure?" *Archaeology Odyssey* 2, no. 3 (July/August 1999): pp. 22–32.

Heimlich, Rüdiger. "The New Trojan War." *Archaeology Odyssey* 5, no. 4 (July/August 2002): pp. 16–23, 55–56.

Hoffman, Barbara. "The Spoils of War." *Archaeology* 46, no. 6 (November/December 1993): pp. 37–40.

Kolb, Frank. "Late Bronze Age Troy: A Response to P. Jablonka and C. B. Rose." AJA Online Publications, January 2005. http://www.ajaonline.org/pdfs/forum/AJA_Kolb_Response_Jan05.pdf.

Korfmann, Manfred. "Was There a Trojan War?" *Archaeology* 57, no. 3 (May/June 2004): pp. 36–41.

Latacz, Joachim. *Troy and Homer: Towards a Solution of an Old Mystery.* Oxford: Oxford University Press, 2004.

Meyer, Karl E. "Who Owns the Spoils of War?" *Archaeology* 48, no. 4 (July/August 1995): pp. 46–59.

Moorehead, Caroline. *Lost and Found: The 9,000 Treasures of Troy: Heinrich Schliemann and the Gold that Got Away.* New York: Penguin Books, 1997.

Robinson, Marcelle. "Pioneer, Scholar, and Victim: An Appreciation of Frank Calvert (1828–1908)." *Anatolian Studies* 44 (1994): pp. 153–168.

Rose, Mark. "What Did Schliemann Find—and Where, When, and How did he find it?" *Archaeology* 46, no. 6 (November/December 1993): pp. 33–36.

Schuchhardt, Carl. *Schliemann's Excavations: An Archaeological and Historical Study.* New York: Macmillan and Co., 1891.

Strauss, Barry. *The Trojan War: A New History.* New York: Simon and Schuster, 2006.

The Truth of Troy. Transcript from BBC Two Documentary, March 25, 2004. From BBC—Science & Nature—Horizon—The Truth of Troy. http://www.bbc.co.uk/science/horizon/2004/troy trans.shtml (accessed September 14, 2009).

Traill, David A. *Excavating Schliemann.* Atlanta, GA: Scholars Press, 1993.

——. "Priam's Treasure: The Story Behind the 4,000-Year-Old Hoard of Trojan Gold." *Archaeology Odyssey* 2, no. 3 (July/August 1999): pp. 14–27, 59.

——. *Schliemann of Troy; Treasure and Deceit.* New York: St. Martin's Griffin, 1995.

——. "Schliemann's 'Discovery' of 'Priam's Treasure.'" *Antiquity* 57 (1983): pp. 181–186.

——, and Igor Bogdanov. "Heinrich Schliemann: Improbable Archaeologist." *Archaeology Odyssey* 2, no. 3 (July/August 1999): pp. 30–39.

Wood, Michael. *In Search of the Trojan War.* Berkeley and Los Angeles: University of California Press, 1998.

From the World Wide Web

At the Museums: Dream to Reality; Treasures from Ancient Syria
http://www.archaeology.org/0107/abstracts/museum.html

"Bones of Contention": The Conflict Between Heinrich Schliemann and Rudolf Virchow in 1880 over the Skeletal Remains from Hanai Tepe
http://www.otago.ac.nz/classics/scholiagfx/v10p054-068.pdf

Excavating Schliemann: Collected Papers on Schliemann | Antiquity | Find Articles at BNET
http://findarticles.com/p/articles/mi_hb3284/is_n259_v68/ai_n28640844/

Troia Project
http://www.uni-tuebingen.de/troia/eng/kontroverse.html

Saudi Aramco World: In Search of the Real Troy
http://www.saudiaramcoworld.com/issue/200501/in.search.of.the.real.troy.htm

Was Troy a Metropolis? Homer Isn't Talking—The New York Times
http://www.nytimes.com/2002/10/22/science/was-troy-a-metropolis-homer-isn-t-talking.html

SOURCE NOTES

(See bibliography on p. 68 for full citations.)

2. Remembering Schliemann

Schliemann's diary entries (listed below) from: Moorehead, Caroline. *Lost and Found: The 9,000 Treasures of Troy: Heinrich Schliemann and the Gold that Got Away.*

> "with black hair and, if possible, beautiful . . ." p. 92.
>
> "I swear she is the only woman . . ." p. 94.
>
> "If you marry me, it must be so . . ." p. 95.
>
> "Have I to take a tent and . . ." p. 88.
>
> "with my flesh creeping and with goose-pimples . . ." p. 101.
>
> "Unfortunately we are obliged to destroy the . . ." p. 112.
>
> "I am among the ruins of Homeric . . ." p. 119.
>
> "I came across a large copper object . . ." p. 130.

3. Troy's Nine Lives

"Although there were some regrettable blunders, those . . ." Blegen, C. W. *Troy and the Trojans,* p. 26.

"The reconstructed Troy seems to have been . . ." Blegen, C. W. *Troy and the Trojans,* p. 89.

"The changes seem to me to be . . ." Blegen, C. W. *Troy and the Trojans,* p. 111.

"As shown by persuasive archaeological evidence, it . . ." Blegen, C. W. *Troy and the Trojans,* p. 162.

4. The Bigger They Are, The Harder They Fall

"Despite assumptions to the contrary, archaeological work . . ." Korfmann, Manfred. "Was There a Trojan War?" *Archaeology* 57, no. 3 (May/June 2004): pp. 36–41.

"In this way the passage of enemy . . ." Latacz, Joachim. *Troy and Homer; Towards a Solution of an Old Mystery,* p. 29.

"We know today, from our own excavations . . ." Korfmann, Manfred. "Was There a Trojan War?": pp. 36–41.

"This gives us a clear idea of . . ." *The Truth of Troy.* Transcript from BBC Two Documentary, March 25, 2004. From BBC—Science & Nature—Horizon—The Truth of Troy. http://www.bbc.co.uk/science/horizon/2004/troytrans.shtml (accessed September 14, 2009).

"The straits . . . are so narrow here . . ." *The Truth of Troy.* Transcript BBC Two Documentary.

"our understanding of ancient Troy from a . . ." Acar, Ozgen, "At the Museums: Dream to Reality," *Archaeology* 54, no. 4 (July/August 2001), http://www.archaeology.org/0107/abstracts/museum.html.

"'Pure fantasy. An archaeological Disneyland,' Kolb accused . . ." Chandler, Graham. "In Search of the Real Troy." Saudi Aramco World (January/February 2005). http://www.saudiaramcoworld.com/issue/200501/in.search.of.the.real.troy.htm.

"Research by Anatolian specialists has shown that . . ." Korfmann, Manfred. "Was There a Trojan War?": pp. 36–41.

"in this area there is no site . . ." Transcript BBC Two Documentary.

"to portray Troy as a center of . . ." Jansen, Hans G., and John Wallrodt, eds. "Controversy over Late Bronze Age Troia (Troia VI and VII)." Troia Project. http://www.uni-tuebingen.de/troia/eng/kontroverse.html.

Quotations from *The Iliad*

The poem is divided into 24 "books." The following list of page numbers is from Samuel Butlers' translation.

Introduction
"[S]leep, love, sweet song and . . .", Book XIII, 636–639.

1. The Legend
"Sing, O goddess, the anger . . .", Book I, 1–7.
". . . the city is given over . . .", Book IX, 590–594.

2. Remembering Schliemann
"My doom has come upon . . .", Book XXII, 300–305.

3. Troy's Nine Lives
"I never recall my word . . .", Book I, 524–527.
"I too shall lie [down] . . ." , Book XVIII, 120–121.

4. The Bigger They Are, The Harder They Fall
"Mighty was the uproar as . . .", Book XIV, 388–406.

ILLUSTRATION AND PHOTO CREDITS

Cover, chapter decorations, map on pages iv–v, and all illustrations in chapter I, copyright © 2011 by Sarah S. Brannen.

M. Gülbiz and Troia Project, University of Tübingen, i; Ancient walls of legendary Troy city © 2011 by Alex Khripunov, used under license from Shutterstock.com, vi.

2. Remembering Schliemann

Schliemann's Excavations (frontispiece), 26; *Schliemann's Excavations* (p. 33), 29; *Schliemann's Excavations* (p. 57), 33; *Schliemann's Excavations* (p. 17), 35.

3. Troy's Nine Lives

Widener Library, Harvard College Library, Arc 522.15 v.I, 38; Photo courtesy of the Department of Classics, University of Cincinnati. Colorized and digitally edited by Rosemary Robertson, 42; Ancient walls of legendary Troy city © 2011 by Alex Khripunov, used under license from Shutterstock.com, 45; Troia Project, University of Tübingen, 47; Photo by Eric H. Cline, 50.

4. The Bigger They Are, The Harder They Fall

Troia Project, University of Tübingen, 52; Troia Project, University of Tübingen, 54; Troia Project, University of Tübingen, 55; Photo courtesy of the Institute of Nautical Archaeology, 59; Troia Project, University of Tübingen and ART+COM AG, Berlin, 61; G. Bieg and Troia Project, University of Tübingen, 62; G. Bieg and Troia Project, University of Tübingen, 63.

Index